LIFE WITH DEATH

Drawings & Life Stories by Child Holocaust Survivors
Compiled & Edited by Tamar Hendel, MA, ATR

CREATE EXPRESSIVE ARTS PRESS
Bethesda, Maryland

CREATE EXPRESSIVE ARTS PRESS

Library of Congress Catalog Card Number 94-69050

Hendel, Tamar
A compilation of drawings and personal histories by Holocaust survivors who were children during World War II

ISBN 0-9655235-0-0

First Edition: October 1996
Printed in Rockville, Maryland by
Phoenix Printing for
CREATE EXPRESSIVE ARTS PRESS
8004-A Norfolk Avenue
Bethesda, Maryland 20814

This book is dedicated to Rebecca, Zalman, Risa and Andy, and Marc and Ann, the next generation.

CONTENTS

i Acknowledgements
ii Foreword
vi Introduction
xiv Presenting the Art Workshop
xv Holly Near's Song

Drawings & Life Stories
1 Steve Attias, "Sacrifice"
2 Marika Barnett, "The Last Night of Hiding in the Coal Bin"
3 Tonia Rotkopf Blair, "The Home We Left Behind, No More They Are"
4 Tonia Rotkopf Blair, "The First View: Extermination"
5 Evi Blaikie, "My Life"
6 Judith Borit, "A Jewish Home in the Time of Holocaust"
7 Theo Brenig, "Last Good-By"
8 Edith Cord, "Why Me?"
9 Maya Freed, "Sorrow/Despair"
10 Alfred Garfinkel, "Life with Death"
11 Betty Ginsburg, "If Not for Them"
12 Leon Ginsburg, "Death Train to Sobibor"
13 Lea Goodman (Apelzon), "A Hole in a Stable on a Polish Farm"
14 Henry Grossman, "Jewish Pool of Genes"
15 Fran Gruber, "It Could Have Been Me"
16 Hans Guggenheim, "We Are Sitting Around a Bare Table"
17 Tamar Hendel, "Dear Grandfather"
18 Amichai Heppner, "Together Again"
19 Helene Herschler, "All Kinds of Fire"
20 Gilberte Hunkind, "I Wish"
21 Zelda Nuss, "It Could Have Been Me, Instead It Was "You" and They Were at Mt. Sinai to Receive the Torah and So Was I"
22 Helen Rothstein, "Hiding & Fighting"
23 Johanna Saper, "My Mother Holding Me As a Baby"
24 Ava Schonberg, "Then & Now"
25 Dana Schwartz, "The Legacy"
26 Ellen Sher, "Where Is Everyone Going"
27 Maurice Singer, "Journey"
28 Eleanor Tannenholz Sobel, "Only One Got Away"
29 Nat Sobel, "Freedom No!"
30 Trudi Alexy Sternlicht, "Triumph Over Guilt"
31 Hedy Van Why, "Ancsika My Lovely Brother: It Could Have Been Me"
32 Rae Weitz, "One Day I'll Be First"

33 Survivor Group Information
34 Order Form

Acknowledgements

My husband, Jacob Fishman, has been a consistent and generous supporter from the start of this project. His enthusiasm and his encouragement have guided me in developing an idea into the reality of a book.

This second collection of drawings owes much to the helpful urging from my friend and fellow member of the Washington/Baltimore Child Survivors group, Erika Rybeck. Had it not been for her determination, suggestions, and good sense, this project may not have gotten a start. Her husband, Walter Rybeck, helped with the editing.

My thanks and appreciation also go to Cheryl Lopez, whose help with the computer and the many revisions was essential. Her time and devotion were generously given despite her many other tasks.

My thanks also goes to Alred Garfinkel who permitted me the use of his drawing on the cover and the title of his picture for the title of the book; to Ed Van Thijn for allowing me to use his speech as the foreword; to Morris Colbert who contributed much time, patience, and expertise; and to Roscoe Lockhart who took on the task of printing at a moment's notice.

I owe my inspiration for the themes of this workshop to Holly Near's song and to the evocative image by the unknown artist whose picture Fran Kahn shared with me.

It is the participants of the workshop who deserve the most thanks. It is because of you, because of us, that this book is possible. Our stories, our histories, stand as witness.

FOREWORD: A HIDDEN CHILD REMEMBERS

By Ed Van Thijn, Mayor of Amsterdam

Until yesterday I didn't know what I had, or rather would be able to say today. Many times I began on, after all, a word of welcome. A hearty welcome, I would say, in Amsterdam, the city of Anne Frank, world symbol of the hidden child, who, exactly fifty years ago, wrote in her diary: "The entrance to our hiding place has now been properly concealed. Mr. Kraler thought it would be better to put a cupboard in front of our door (because a lot of houses are being searched for hidden bicycles), but of course it had to be a movable cupboard that can open like a door."

Naturally, everyone has long been familiar with the story of Anne Frank, but Anne Frank did not survive the War and we, luckily, did. We were allowed to speak of luck which is why we rarely if ever spoke.

But even among the survivors, the tale of the child who was "only" hidden takes just a modest place. On the world ranking list of Holocaust misery we score only a few modest points.

Besides, with whom were we actually supposed to speak? Who was prepared to hear the story which so totally dominated our lives, our existence, but that we -- at least most of us -- desperately wanted, or had to, or tried to, suppress, because we had to go on with everyday life which resumed its normal or abnormal pace. I, myself had the great good fortune that both my parents survived the War, but that did not mean that they were ready to listen to my story. Understandably so. My father needed all his unrestrained energy -- and I think back on him with wonder -- to fight -- without any training -- for his own independent existence. My mother was traumatized -- we would say today -- by her own War experiences, the loss of her entire family, the dislocation of her household (mostly following the War) and the dread she had endured during the years of separation from her only child. Because of me, in other words. I cannot say that the subject "War" was taboo at home. It was just the opposite. But -- it sounds cynical -- it was "her" war, not "my" war with which I was confronted daily. From first generation I rapidly became second generation.

With whom were we supposed to speak, with professionals? I saw plenty. I was namely a problem case. I had severe asthma, spent a lot of time in bed, was difficult, unbearable, and exceptionally unmanageable. I was dragged to dozens of doctors, specialists, even a child psychiatrist. I underwent the craziest treatments, including electroshock. Not once did the subject of the War come up. Never once did one of those brilliant minds ask me to tell my story. The "Conspiracy of Silence" about which Dr. Yael Danieli the famous traumatic stress scholar, published, is an absolute fact.

With whom could you have spoken? With your peers? Classmates, school friends, boyfriends, girlfriends? We had no peers. We lived in totally different worlds, no matter how communicative we were. On the one hand you were much older that others your age, more experienced, sadder and wiser. While on the other hand you were many years younger because of all that you had missed, because you had never been to school, and had never played outside. And what would they make of your story? If, on occasion, in an unguarded or intimate moment, you told something of your personal history, a deep silence would descend as if you had spoken in an incomprehensible dialect.

Oddly enough, I had similar experiences with my Jewish friends. We never spoke of our experiences. Dozens of years later I would discover that some of my most intimate friends were rescued by the same resistance organization and that we had been hidden practically next door to each other.

Your own children then, many years later? That has given me the greatest possible difficulty. How do you tell your children, when, at what age? And what will you tell them? Bibeb, one of the few journalists to whom I dared lift a corner of the veil, wrote the following story in '75:

> "This summer I got up my nerve to visit Westerbork for the first time. They had erected that gorgeous monument. The spur line, the tracks. I went with my children. So often I've tried to explain it to them ... Still it was a big disappointment for them, something like: Well is that all ... The oldest began to balance on the rails. My first reaction was disillusionment. The second: relief. My oldest daughter, at exactly the age I was when I was walking there ... was playing a game. Dammit, isn't that fantastic. I though: What utter madness to try to talk to her about all that wretchedness.

Westerbork. I realize that I still haven't told you my story. And that's what we're here for. At last, here goes. I had eighteen different hiding addresses, but my tale begins and ends in Westerbork. I will tell it telegram style. In March '43 my mother and I were taken from our home and brought to Westerbork. There I spent several months, primarily in the hospital barrack. Thanks to my father, who with a number other men had jumped out of the train earlier (he had a train key), we learned in the night that our name had been called to return to Amsterdam. This was followed by immediate admission to the New Israel Hospital on the Nieuwe Keizersgracht, in the contagious disease ward (that instilled fear). After a week there was a new raid. The hospital would be evacuated. In the middle of the raid my father plucked us out of the hospital in a stolen ambulance and, a few street corners away, in the middle of the night, handed me over to a total stranger, a woman who, it later turned out, was with the NV-organization. She brought me with the first train to Brunssum. A hiding across eighteen addresses, first in Limburg, after that in Overijsel, followed. Some addresses were good for three days. Others for two months. All the addresses were totally different. Almost all the families were deeply religious, but one was Roman Catholic, the next strict Dutch Reformed. Everywhere -- it goes without saying -- I had to fit in right away and participate in the customary rituals from one day to the next. This did not cause me much trouble. One time, however, it got too much for me, for a completely banal reason ... For several weeks I had been living in a Catholic household, and I had already completely identified myself with Catholicism, when the day of my tenth birthday arrived. I came early to the breakfast table, awaiting the events that would follow. But nothing happened at all. When I asked if they knew that it was my birthday, they said, "Yes, but we don't celebrate birthdays. We only celebrate Saints days." I burst into tears and screamed, "What a rotten belief!" That same day I was back on the street. Seven more addresses would follow, now in Overijsel. At my eighteenth address I was captured. That was on a farm in Oudleusen, November 1944. The first time they searched for hours but found nothing. The second time they walked straight to the cupboard where I was hidden.

A clear example of betrayal. I then spent two months in the detention center in Zwolle, four to a cell. In January '45 I was taken to Westerbork, all that time to the nightmare I knew so well. But everything was different. The ten-thousands from before were not there anymore. In April I, along with the few hundred who were still there, was freed by the Canadians.

So that's the story. Talk about luck.

I want to end with three observations. About identity. About gratitude. And about the ability of children to remember.

About identify. My identity lies locked in my personal life story. I learned to pray and think in so many diverse religions, that in the end I inevitably decided to go my own way. I will let nothing and no-one prescribe how I wish to identify myself and I am averse to any kind of collective labeling. But I have a deep respect of those who have made another choice. From all my experiences with all those diverse religions I have not retained anything negative. On the contrary. I learned to respect people of all different beliefs. The tolerance for which I try in my present position to stand was, in truth, poured into me in childhood.

About gratitude. "Why do I have to be grateful?" I overheard one of us call out desperately, "What were their motives? I've become very distrustful." I found that a shocking statement, but it is a subject with which many of us wrestle. Years ago I put this problem before one of my teachers, Professor Presser, after he had interviewed me for his book The Destruction of the Dutch Jews. To so many rescuers who risked their lives, so many families who ran into danger, cell mates who pampered me, I am permanently in debt. Presser's answer was enlightening. "Naturally," he said, "you must feel gratitude, but it is impossible to order your life on the basis of gratitude. Children don't do that toward their own parents who brought them into the world either." Members of the NV-group, the resistance organization which rescued 210 children, myself among them, reacted in the same way when I asked them if they would mind if we would nominate them for recognition by Yad Vashem. "We don't want any recognition. We don't want any, thank you very much. We are more than rewarded by the fact that you survived and found your way in life." We cannot order our lives on the basis of gratitude, it shouldn't become an obsession, but we can, all things being equal, harbor feelings of respect and gratitude for those who stuck their necks out for us, while others (most) stood by, whatever their motives may have been.

We, the children of the NV-group, after much deliberation, persisted in our resolve to get the Yad Vashem recognition after all, but it was not any easy task. Since we insisted, the NV-group wanted to be recognized collectively, also to honor their leaders (such as Jaap Musch and Joop Woortman, for whom a square has just been named) who did not survive the War. But it wasn't that simple. The regulations of Israeli recognition go out to heroic individuals, "The Righteous." The problem could only be solved if we could find forty personal eye-witnesses to testify as to the behavior of all twenty members of the NV-group, two witnesses per person.

And that brings me to my last observation: about a child's ability to remember. Let me assure you that it was one hell of a job to collect those forty witnesses. First of all we had to find them. Fortunately a list existed somewhere. But once found they had to be willing to cooperate. The terrified reactions were initially enormous. "What? How do you know that? I'm on a list?" Others, furious, hung up the phone. "I don't want to hear any more about that." Still others were willing to help out but never succeeded in getting anything down on paper. Eventually there were forty eyewitness reports on the table. Elated we marched to the Embassy where, to our utter amazement, we were told the following: "Forty eye-witnesses, but sir, they are all children's stories. That's no good to us. They are completely worthless." To make a long story short: the Yad Vashem recognition was finally granted, but if there is one thing that has infuriated me in the past years it is that as a child I was often not taken seriously.

With whom could we have spoken? With just about no-one. And if, on some rare occasion, we mustered all our courage to tell something of our story, we were met with disbelief and told: "What are you talking about? May I ask how old you were then?"

Now, almost fifty years after our hiding, make at least one thing clear. Never underestimate children. We know: children are sometimes real people. No matter how young they may be, they will always remember traumatic experiences. Let the world think carefully about that before turning their eyes away from all the children who today are in flight from the ethnic cleansing in Sarajevo or from the famine in Somalia.

Excerpted from speech delivered on August 23, 1992, in Amsterdam at the Hidden Child conference.

(Translated by F. V. Kan)

INTRODUCTION: HOW THIS BOOK OF PICTURES CAME TO BE

This collection of pictures by child survivors of the Holocaust is a result of my professional interest in art making as an art therapist. Since I am also a child survivor, I am always aware of the unfinished emotional business in our lives. As part of my art therapy training many years ago, I drew several pictures about my feelings regarding World War II and about the effect of those times on my life.

One Sunday afternoon in 1986, I brought two of the drawings to a meeting of the Washington/Baltimore Child Survivors of the Holocaust. I had been attending these monthly meetings since shortly after the group was formed. We have been coming together month after month since then.

The first meetings were difficult. For many months we were not sure how to conduct them. We had much heated discussion about whether to organize ourselves with rules and procedures or to remain an informal social group; whether to create a formal national organization bringing all the other groups meeting across the nation in other large cities together, or to remain unique in our own "family."

We had no difficulty with our concept of "family" -- we considered each other siblings who had finally come to know each other. And like family get-togethers, each of our meetings began with a pot luck meal. After the meal we shared our stories.

Unlike a kindergarten show & tell, we did not bring a special gift or a joyful family holiday trip to tell about. The events we talked about were childhood experiences, which 50 years ago, we had no kindly kindergarten class to share with. Our childhood memories were hard to imagine and hard to describe, and many of us avoided talking about them. At our meetings we gave each other (and ourselves) permission to do so. But they are not stories that can be told in one sitting. Memories have layers and implications to relationships to others of one's family, both long ago and in the present. I had made my two drawings in 1976; but at that time, when my children were young, I was not ready to dwell on their meaning and put them away.

We are now a group of about 100, born mostly between the years 1925 and 1942. During World War II we were either children or young teenagers. Some of us had been in concentration camps. Some of us were separated from our parents and hidden by non-Jewish families or organizations. Some of us were fortunate in that we remained, even in hiding, with our parents, one or both of whom survived. All of us lost many family members. In that respect we were not different from the Jewish adults who experienced the war. Yet we regarded our experience as different from theirs. Many of our meetings were consumed pondering those differences. Again and again, as each of us told our stories, we recognized how significantly unique those wartime events were for us. They shaped us, since we were children at that time.

One of our members, Erika Rybeck, wrote:

We sift through the ashes of our past
Children no more
Yet searching forever
For the lost years
For the lost tears
For the lost faces
For the lost places
Of our lost childhood.

Even now many of us are still hiding the depth and breadth of the feelings from our childhood, from ourselves, from our children, from our spouses. And here we are, well into our middle age and beyond.

How should we reconstruct a childhood that wasn't a childhood? How could we bring a voice out of hiding that is out of practice, that doesn't know whether to speak or not? In order to protect us, our parents minimized what happened to us since we were "just children." When we came here after the war, our relatives and others in this country did not know how to respond to us, and sometimes did not want to hear what we had to say. Their well-meaning advice was to forget the past and to look to the future. We, ourselves, were doing just that -- being busy with our lives, becoming "normal," getting married, having children. We put behind us the enormity of the injury done us.

What I now know, both personally and as a result of my training and experience as an art therapist, is that those of us who have been hurt as children need a very special atmosphere in which to tell our story. It is not enough only to tell the story. As children, we needed to howl and scream. We wanted to rage and shout our anger. We needed to mourn our endless losses but had no words to name them. In order to now divulge the full extent of our pain and sorrow, those of us who are willing to tell our stories need to know that we will be listened to, that we will be believed and understood, that we will be comforted. Because beyond the telling are the feelings, and we had not known how and to whom to express those feelings. And now that it is time to mourn, or perhaps to "resurrect" the children we were, we needed witnesses. In our coming together we are each other's witnesses.

I did not know what it was I wanted to accomplish that day when I brought my drawings to the meeting. Something had felt stuck for me and needed to become unstuck. I half hoped and half knew that now I could bring out of hiding feelings that, like the pictures, had been put away for many years.

Both drawings had been done as part of my training in Art Therapy at George Washington University in Washington, D.C. In order to master the skill of leading groups of patients in the psychotherapeutic process of learning about themselves, it is important for the art therapy students to take on the role of group participants themselves. It was in such an art therapy training group that I drew the first two pictures.

The first, titled "HALT," started as a scribble. (PLATE I) A scribble is an art therapy device that helps difficult or forgotten memories and feelings to emerge. By relaxing momentarily with a few stretches and wide arm movements, one prepares oneself for drawing random spontaneous lines on a large sheet of paper. After observing the lines and shapes from several angles, giving one's imagination free reign, objects and shapes begin to appear, much as they do when one looks for pictures in clouds. Then, other lines, shapes and colors are added to the drawing to more fully develop the image. The extraneous lines are allowed to remain. Much to my surprise, the picture that emerged from my scribble was the face of Hitler with his arm forward and the palm up -- a signal for "Halt." This picture is about my anger that my life had been halted and disrupted by the Nazis, and also about my helplessness and powerlessness. Drawing it brought back the memories of the incredible fear I experienced.

A couple of incidents come to mind. I am walking with my mother. She is young and beautiful, stylishly dressed as always. I have on my pretty sailor dress and a white bow in my hair. We are two ladies taking an evening stroll. But it must be getting late, for my mother uses her hand bag to hide the yellow star pinned to her dress and nervously urges us to hurry home. It is almost curfew time, time for Jews to be off the streets.

The second is a memory from April, 1941. My mother and I are on a train, leaving Zagreb, Yugoslavia. My father has paid a man who is a member of the Ustase (the Yugoslav Fascist organization) to pose as the husband/father, and smuggle us out of the country. The train conductor comes to collect the tickets and asks us, "Are you Jews?" My mother and I are silent. After an eternity, the man says, "no" and the conductor passes on. That moment is forever imprinted in my mother's memory. Over the years, she tells and retells the story of the fear in my eyes as I quietly look at her. At any moment anyone could come up to me and worst of all for a child, to my strong and beautiful mother, and say, "HALT!" Not only had my safety been shattered, but also the safety that comes to each child from believing in her parents' ability to protect her from harm. I felt my mother's fear and knew that she was as powerless and as helpless as I.

The second picture, "SOLINGEN," is about both rage and fear. (PLATE II) Solingen is a famous brand of German knives. The subject had come up in my family in America about purchasing knives for the kitchen and I had not wanted to get those particular ones because they were German-made. It was after this discussion that I drew the picture.

A large bloody knife with the word Solingen holds center stage in the drawing. Behind it is a black wire fence and behind the fence are two figures. I, as the red figure, have just stabbed the black figure. But there is some ambivalence. My hand is not on the knife. Am I really the killer I imagine I can be? For many years I had been asking myself this question. Would I have been able to kill in order to protect my life or the life

HALT

Soligen

of someone I loved, like my child, or my parent? Would I have been willing to kill "the enemy" whoever they were and wherever I found them, as "they" were willing and able to kill my family and me? My rage and wish to kill and bludgeon became so strong at one point that I frightened myself. I had begun to think that indeed I was capable of killing and this realization terrified me, but it also brought me a sense of understanding. Having discovered my own blood lust, I understand better how victims can become perpetrators and I fear for the inheritors of war and violence everywhere. Though we cannot but hope that the Holocaust was an aberration, we know in light of recent history that "racial cleansing" is alive and well in many parts of the world. So regularly is one group victimized by another, it is no surprise that reprisals and counter reprisals occur everywhere regularly. I have greater respect now for the years of teaching we humans need in order to master peacefulness. It is a miracle, I believe, each time we do not take an eye for an eye, each time we act graciously and kindly one to another.

I had not elaborated much on these thoughts except with other child survivors. The impact of these pictures on the group when I told about them was such that several members asked to join me in drawing and talking about our childhood experiences.

During 1988, several of us met about six times to draw and talk together and thus we began the first in a series of Art Workshops.

One of my drawings from that first Art Workshop is entitled "DON'T LOOK ... DON'T SEE ... DON'T FEEL ... DON'T SAY." (PLATE III) It was drawn in response to an incident that occurred in Rome, probably in the spring of 1944. The American armies had been bombing Rome fairly regularly. My extended family was in hiding. The adults were not working. The children were not attending school. Many of our days were organized around picnicking on the steps of St. Peter's Cathedral, or some parks in that area, because it was well known that St. Peter's would not be bombed. Returning home one evening, we walked past part of the city that had been bombed just a short time before. The injured people had already been taken away, but a dead horse, whose exploded remains had been flung about, was still there. My mother grabbed me, and my aunt grabbed my cousin, each saying to us, "Don't look!" As in the picture, our eyes were shielded, but not totally. How could we not have looked?

Surely we wished we had not seen! That image haunted my cousin for years. As a boy, he remembers being frightened by rhythmic sounds coming from behind him, turning around slowly, to make sure it was not that bloody headless horse.

Surely our mothers wished we had not seen it. As painful as it is for children to see one's parents frightened and powerless, being a mother I know how painful it is for a parent to be unable to protect one's child. How much simpler to think that our young age protected us from being aware of what was happening. How natural for our parents and other adults to tell us, "Don't look. Don't talk. Enough is enough!" After awhile it didn't have to be said to us. We, ourselves, went on to other things. And now those hidden memories, like the hidden children we were, are coming out of hiding. We want to look, to see, to feel, to say.

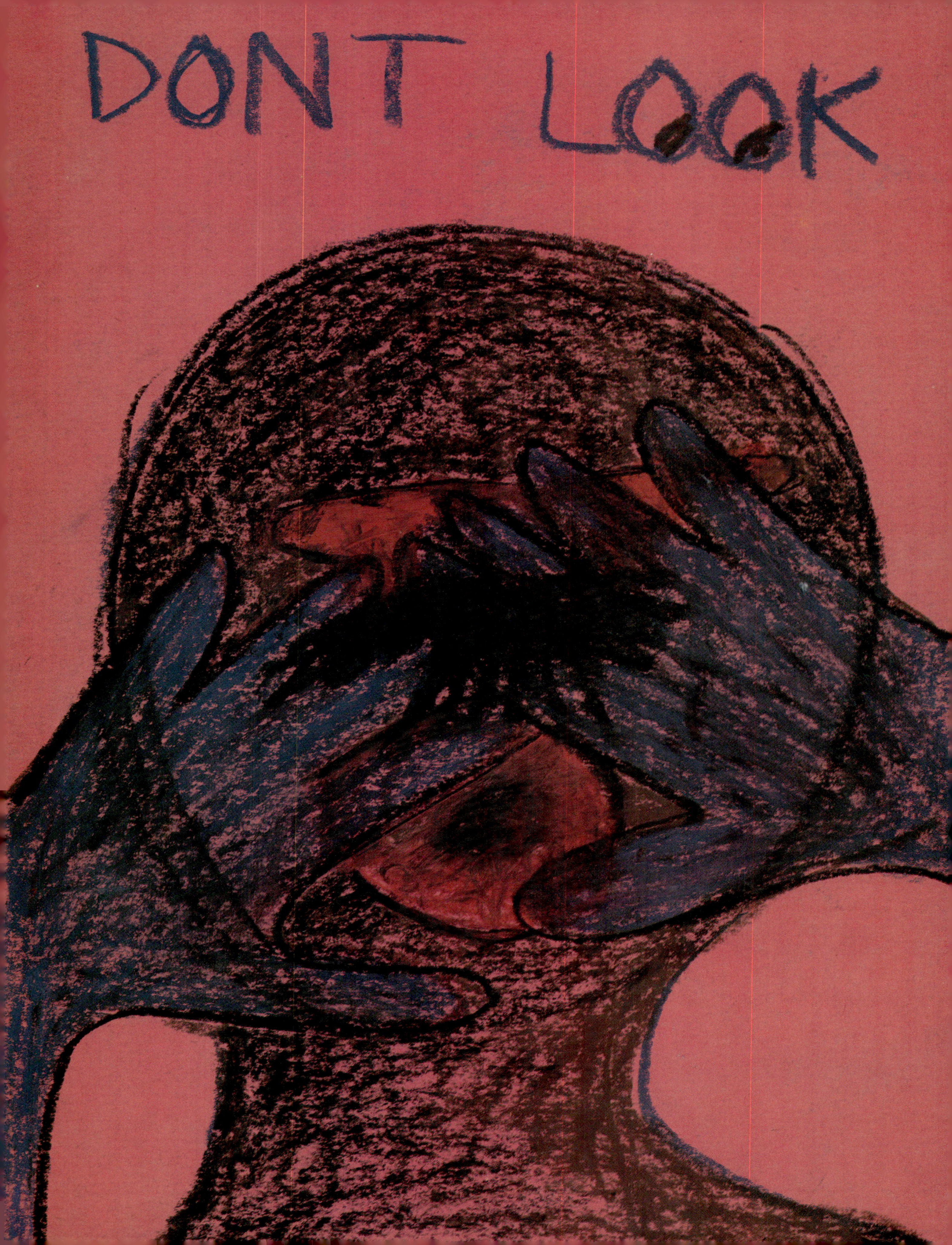
DONT LOOK

The last few years, much has been written by Holocaust survivors. I have included most of the address presented to the Hidden Child Conference in Amsterdam in 1993 by Ed Van Thijn. He is a child survivor and was then the Mayor of Amsterdam. His words so aptly describe the experience of the child in hiding and all the questions that we have puzzled over since those times.

It would be a mistake to think that because some of the adult survivors and some of the child survivors have been so eloquent, and so articulate in writing about the Holocaust experience, that it suffices. Each of us needs to tell others our stories in order to unlock our own hearts to the enormity of the pain and the loss we can hardly bear. When we draw our pictures and tease out the memories and the stories and the feelings, it is so that we do not walk about in our life, not knowing why, from time to time, we feel like crying or shouting or hiding.

It is understandable that Mr. Ed Van Thijn, when speaking to a large audience, needed to speak "in telegram style." Many of us have been speaking "in telegram style" about our childhood experiences for years. Our families meant to help us when they praised us for our stoic demeanor, but they did not. I hope that, like those of us who attend smaller gatherings, Mr. Van Thijn has also had the opportunity to speak among friends and to speak of his feelings.

Telling one's stories is no small undertaking. As Isaac Dinesen has written, sorrow is better borne when told in a story. But the emphasis needs to be on told, told with feeling, told with tears, and heard with open arms.

The Art Workshops have served us well. It has been hard for us to speak of our childhood. We have been holding back the tears for a long time. By eliciting, collecting, and presenting these drawings, we have had the opportunity to hear and to be heard. We have added our testimony as witnesses for our family members who are no longer here to speak for themselves, and for our children -- some of whom are afraid to ask or don't know what and how to ask about their family history. If there are others like ourselves who sometimes hold back the tears, knowing something needs to be told yet not sure how to begin, I hope this book may serve them well also.

Washington, D.C.
Tamar Hendel, M.A., A.T.R.

PRESENTING THE ART WORKSHOP

I first heard Holly Near sing, "It Could Have Been Me But It Was You," many years ago. I was alone driving in my car and was profoundly moved by the words of the song. I cried and cried, tears blurring my vision as I continued to drive on my way to the grocery store.

Holly Near's song was written at a time of conflict and strain in this country which culminated in the killing of students at Kent State University. But for me, those words brought back another time in history when my family and I, and millions more, were caught in a different upheaval, one that caused us to lose our homes, our loved ones, and our pride.

When I became a member of the Washington/Baltimore group of Child Survivors of the Holocaust many years later, I learned that I was not unique in thinking that I was spared at the expense of others dying. Nor was I alone in my sense of guilt at having survived while others had not. When for the first time I heard the words, "It could have been me but instead it was you," it evoked images for me of my grandfather and uncle who were shot as hostages in 1941 shortly after we escaped from Zagreb, Yugoslavia, and of my aunts, uncles, and cousins from Yugoslavia and Poland who perished in Auschwitz.

For the 1991 National Conference of Child Survivors of the Holocaust, I had been requested to offer an art workshop for the members of the group. In my search for a suitable theme for the workshop, I chose to present Holly Near's song, knowing it would elicit powerful memories and feelings in others as it had in me. I chose also to show a picture given me recently by a member of the Washington/Baltimore group, Fran Kahn, who had found it in the newspaper. (We never did discover who the artist is.) The symbolism of barbed wire turning into freely-flying birds was most appropriate for us all.

The words of the song and the drawing were enlarged and displayed. I described the theme to the participants, played the tape of the song, and invited everyone to sing it with me. Each person was then invited to draw in their own way, a picture of their response to the theme and a brief explanation to go with the drawing. Each participant's story was spontaneously written during the workshop and not changed afterwards, except in minor ways. Some of the histories, which were contributed later, were shortened in order for both the story and the history to fit on one page.

The participants in the workshop for the most part are not artists, although some are. Because the experiences that are described happened when we were children, some of the picture styles reflect this; although at the time of the workshop, those of us who are survivors were in our 50's and 60's, and some of our children were in their 20's and 30's.

Both of the art works - the song and the picture, were presented to elicit memories and thoughts which we are reluctant to allow ourselves when we are alone or with people who have not had our experiences. When we are together at meetings or conferences, we are better able to share these painful feelings and comfort each other. Though the memories never go away, after a time of remembering together, we begin to feel less alone in the world.

It Could Have Been Me
By Holly Near

It could have been me
But instead it was you
So I'll keep doing the things
you were doing
As if I were two.

I'll be a lover of life
A singer of songs
A farmer of food
A righter of wrongs.

It could have been me
But instead it was you
And it may be we, dear
brothers & sisters
Before we are through.

But if you can work for freedom
Freedom, freedom, freedom
If you can work for freedom
I can too.

SACRIFICE

BY STEVE ATTIAS

THE NAZIS SELECT THE CHILDREN TODAY. A MOTHER PLEADS WITH THE SS GUARD TO TAKE HER LIFE INSTEAD OF HER DAUGHTER'S.

THE GUARD OBLIGES.

FOR THE REST OF HER LIFE "SHE" CARRIES THE BURDEN FOR TWO.

SACRIFICE

The Nazi's select the children
today. A mother pleads with
the SS guard to take Her
life instead of Her daughter's.

The Guard obliges...

For the rest of her life
"she" carries the burden for
two.

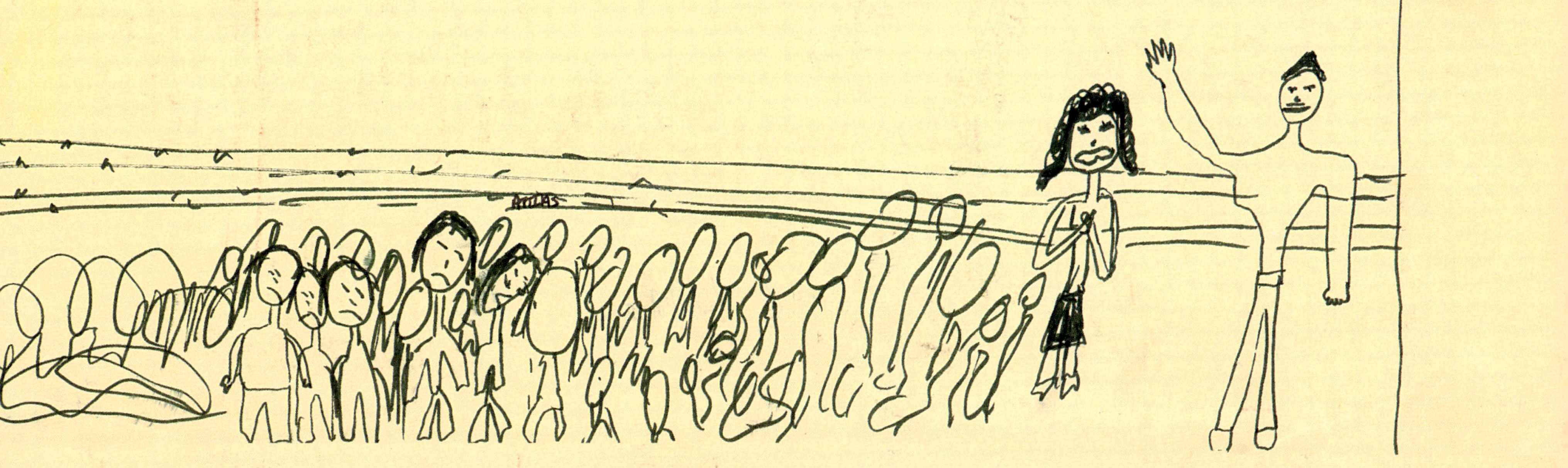

THE LAST NIGHT OF HIDING IN THE COAL BIN

BY MARIKA BARNETT

WE HAD TO SURVIVE JUST ONE MORE NIGHT. THE RUSSIANS - FIGHTING FROM HOUSE TO HOUSE - WERE APPROACHING THE BUILDING WHERE MY PARENTS AND I WERE HIDING. THE COAL BIN WAS COLD IN JANUARY, ALL THE LITTLE WINDOWS THAT LOOKED ONTO THE COURTYARD WERE BROKEN. THERE WERE BRICKS IN THE COURTYARD AND EVERYONE ASKED THE MEN TO PILE UP THE BRICKS IN FRONT OF THE WINDOWS. THE MEN, LIKE MY FATHER, WERE WEAK FROM HUNGER AND REFUSED TO BRAVE THE FREEZING WEATHER TO BLOCK THE WINDOWS. THAT NIGHT THE RUSSIANS ENTERED OUR BUILDING BY THROWING A SMALL BOMB THROUGH THE GATE. THE EXPLOSION TORE OPEN FIVE FLOORS ABOVE AND BURIED EVERYONE ALIVE IN THE BOMB SHELTER. ONLY GENTILES WERE ALLOWED INTO THE SHELTER. THEY ALL PERISHED. THE FUMES OF THE EXPLOSION SPREAD SLOWLY. IT GOT INTO THE SECTION WHERE WE WERE. WE EXPECTED TO DIE. I WAS KNEELING IN FRONT OF MY MOTHER AND BURIED MY HEAD INTO HER LAP. SHE HELD ME TIGHT AND WE EXPECTED TO SUFFOCATE SLOWLY FROM THE GAS. AFTER A WHILE, I LOOKED UP AND WONDERED IF I AM STILL ALIVE. WE ALL WERE. THANKS TO THE LAZINESS OF OUR MEN, THE GAS QUICKLY EVAPORATED THROUGH THE BROKEN WINDOWS.

I was born in January, 1934, in Budapest, Hungary. Our family consisted of my parents, me, and an older half-sister who got married and left for America in 1939. My mother came from a very large, wealthy family and I spent all my summers at my maternal grandparents' house in the northeast corner of Hungary. In 1944, they were all shipped to Auschwitz. Only one cousin returned, but soon she was sentenced to 25 years of forced labor in Siberia. A few other cousins survived in Budapest. Two aunts moved in with us and since their own family was killed, they stayed with us for the rest of their lives. I was hiding with gentiles, then in a convent, and eventually I was hidden along with my parents and aunts by the Jewish underground. In between my various hiding places, I was living with my parents in a so-called "Wallenberg Safe-house." While I was in the convent, my parents escaped four times as they were led to the Collection Center at the railroad station or to be executed at the shore of the Danube. Once Roul Wallenberg saved them.

The last night of Hiding in the coalbin.

Marika Barnett

THE HOME WE LEFT BEHIND
NO MORE THEY ARE

BY TONIA ROTKOPF BLAIR

MOTHER, FATHER, OLDER SISTER, YOUNGER BROTHER ... LOVE, WARMTH, CARING.

I am Tonia Rotkopf Blair, daughter of Mendel and Miriam Gitla, from Lodz, Poland.

One day in March, 1940, when I was training as a nurse away from home, (hiding my real age of 14), I saw my parents, my 16-year old sister, and my 11-year old brother, being marched to the train by German soldiers with hundreds of other Jews. I never saw them again.

Some time later, I did receive mail from them marked, Mszana Dolna, until Summer, 1942.

In 1980, I discovered the ravine, overlooking the town of Mszana Dolna, where my whole family in a group of 881 children, women and men, were shot to death on August 19, 1942.

I was a nurse in Lodz Ghetto Hospital, shipped to Auschwitz in 1944, transported to slave labor at Freiburg, liberated in Mauthausen.

I live with my husband, Vachel, in New York City, and have two grown sons - Doniphan and Nicholas, and a 12-year old granddaughter, Irena.

No More
They Are

Tonia

THE FIRST VIEW: EXTERMINATION

BY TONIA ROTKOPF BLAIR

THE TRAIN STOPPED WITH A CLANKING OF STEEL ON STEEL.

IT WAS QUIET AS WE ALMOST STOPPED BREATHING.

WHAT NEXT.

A TINY WINDOW VERY HIGH NEAR THE CEILING OF THE TRAIN ALLOWED SOME DAYLIGHT IN.

FIRST, ONE PERSON CLIMBED ON THE BACK OF THE KNEELING, YOUNG MAN TO CHECK WHAT WAS OUTSIDE.

NO ONE SPOKE.

IT WAS MY TURN.

THE AREA WAS VAST.

IT LOOKED FOREBODING.

THE DESOLATION WAS ALMOST COMPLETE.

THEN WE FACED IT.

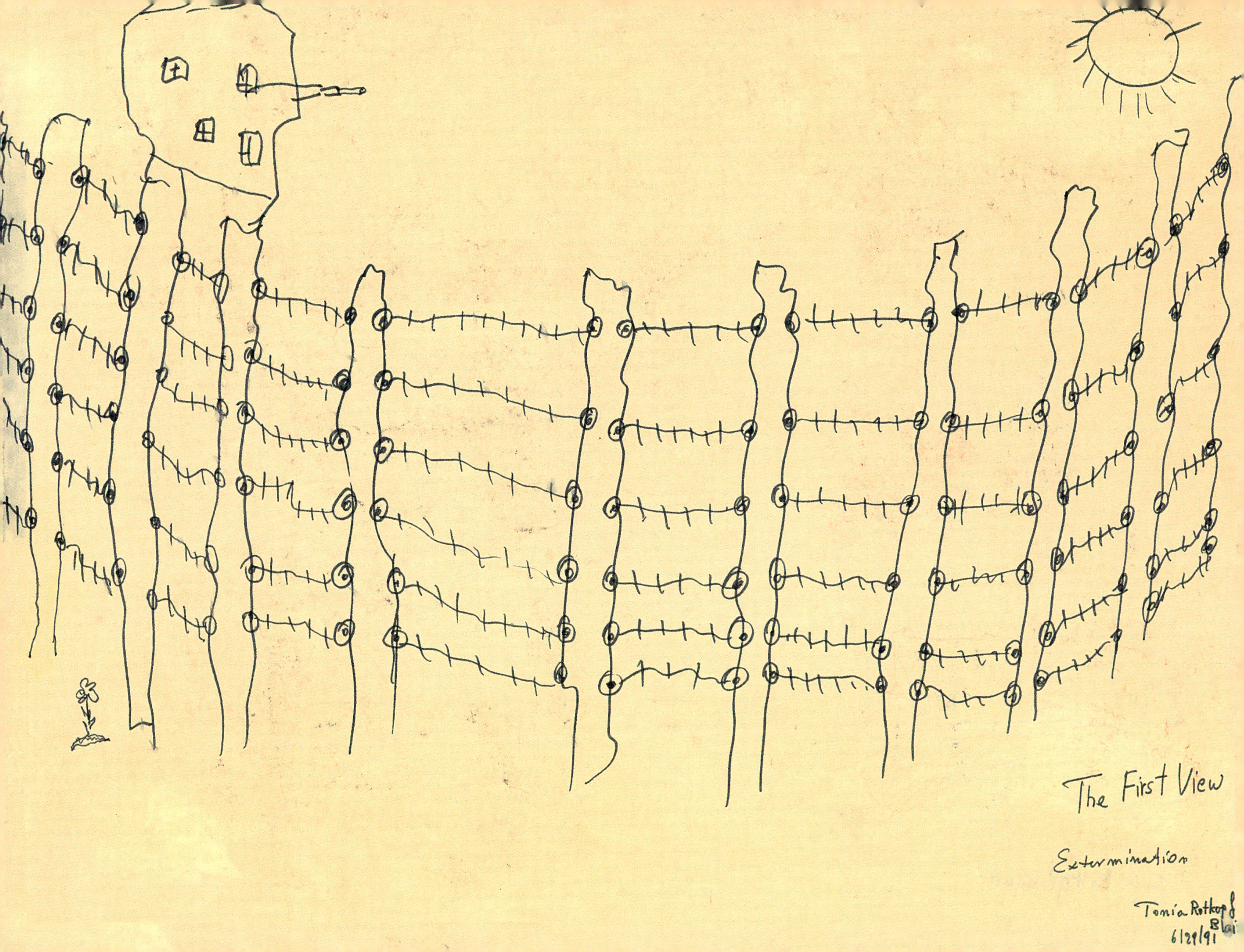
The First View
Extermination
Tonia Rotkopf Blai
6/29/91

MY LIFE

BY EVI BLAIKIE

A DISJOINTED, UGLY, ANGRY,
BRUTAL AND THORNY
BEGINNING. IT SLOWLY GETS
SMOOTHER AND BETTER. SOME
JOY EVEN COMES INTO IT. BUT
THE SEEDS FROM THE
BEGINNING CANNOT BE
STAMPED OUT.

I was born in Paris, France, to Hungarian immigrants in January 1939. When the Germans invaded France in 1941, both my parents were deported ... my father to Auschwitz, my mother to a slave labor camp. An aunt took me to Hungary to be with the rest of my family. When the Germans marched into Hungary in March 1944, we were confined to a "Jewish House." A maid smuggled my cousin and me to a farm where we spent the remainder of the war, living with false identities. My father, along with my grandparents and uncles, died in Auschwitz. My mother survived and we returned to France together, eventually emigrated to England, where I went to school. I came to New York City in 1960, married, had three children. I still live in the city and work as an apparel designer.

MY LIFE
EVI-BLAIKIEK

A JEWISH HOME IN THE TIME OF HOLOCAUST

(ONE OF A SERIES)

BY JUDITH BORIT

HOLOCAUST AND WAR - A DEFINING EXPERIENCE. THIS PICTURE REMINDS ME OF THE FIRST TWO PICTURES I HAVE MADE IN PREVIOUS ANNUAL GATHERINGS. MY GUESS IS I AM ATTEMPTING TO INTERPRET MORE FULLY MY CHILDHOOD EXPERIENCES AND IN PARTICULAR THE DESTRUCTION, CHAOS OF THE WAR AND HOLOCAUST. THIS IS ONE PICTURE IN A SERIES. TITLE OF THE SERIES IS "JEWISH HOME." AT OUR NEXT GATHERING I'LL HAVE SOME OF THE EARLIER PICTURES TOO.

I was born in Budapest Hungary, the second of three children, into a practicing Jewish family. When the Nazis overran Hungary in March of 1944, I was eight years old. My father's father died just a few months before. We still attended a private school where we studied German and English! All schools closed in Budapest at that time and for us Jews, the awful times accelerated. I was relatively lucky - all my immediate family in Budapest survived and we lived out the war together. For us kids that was very lucky.

Most of the war I spent with my family in a Swiss-protected make-shift Jewish hospital, which was a Jewish elementary school before, just in front of the ghetto walls.

My red-headed cousin a little younger than I, was killed with all of his family in Auschwitz.

jewish home in the time of holocaust

B

Jewish home during the time of holocaust
Judy Borit
6-29-91

LAST GOOD-BY

BY THEO BRENIG

IN 1942 MY PARENTS AND I WERE IN THE CAMP DES MILLES IN SOUTHERN FRANCE. ON AUGUST 10 DEPORTATIONS TO NORTHERN FRANCE AND ULTIMATELY TO AUSCHWITZ BEGAN. THE FRENCH AT THAT TIME DID NOT DEPORT CHILDREN UNDER 16 YEARS OF AGE. THE PICTURE REPRESENTS ME LEAVING THE CAMP ON A BUS WITH MANY OTHER CHILDREN. I AM LEANING OUT OF THE WINDOW AND HOLDING HANDS WITH MY FATHER, NOT KNOWING WHAT WAS GOING TO HAPPEN TO HIM AND IF WE WILL EVER MEET AGAIN. I NEVER SAW HIM AGAIN.

I was born in Vienna, Austria, on July 17, 1927. In February 1939, my parents, brother and I left for Belgium. In May 1940, my father was arrested by the Belgians and went through several French camps ending up in the Camp Des Milles in unoccupied Southern France. We followed him in 1941 and my mother and I were interned in the Hotel Terminus Du Port in Marseille. In August of 1942, my parents were deported to Auschwitz and killed on arrival. My brother escaped and stayed in the French underground. I was placed in a childrens home run by the OSE, the Chateau Du Masgelier. In September 1943, I escaped to Switzerland and lived first in the Childrens Homes Les Murailles and La Foret. I became an engineer and came to the U.S. in 1961. I have lived in Lynchburg, Virginia, ever since. My brother lives in New York.

LAST GOOD-BY

TB 6/29/91

WHY ME?

BY EDITH CORD

I ALWAYS ASKED MYSELF WHY I SURVIVED AND, MORE, WHAT I HAVE TO DO TO JUSTIFY MY LIFE: DO SOMETHING SPECIAL? SAVE THE WORLD? OR WHAT? GRADUALLY I REALIZED THAT I CAN LIVE AN ORDINARY LIFE AND, IN THAT ORDER, WENT TO SCHOOL, LEARNED AGAIN TO PLAY AND HAVE FUN, AND WORK - LIKE EVERYONE ELSE. THOSE WHO PERISHED WOULD HAVE WANTED THAT FOR US. SO OUR LIVES ARE A TRIBUTE TO THEM AS WELL AS AN AFFIRMATION OF LIFE. L'CHAYIM!

I was born in Vienna, Austria. In 1937, we moved to Italy. We were kicked out of Italy in 1938 and succeeded in crossing illegally into France where we received political asylum. When France was occupied by the Germans in June 1940, my father was arrested along with my 17-year old brother. They were taken to the Camp in Gurs, then Rivesaltes. My father was deported in October 1942. Though my brother escaped from the camp, he eventually was also deported in September 1942. Both were murdered in Auschwitz. In 1943, I went into hiding. I was hidden in various schools and a convent. I was in thirteen places in eleven months. In May 1944, I joined a group of thirty other Jewish children and we crossed into Switzerland illegally. In 1952 I came to the U.S. My mother joined me in 1953. I am married, have three grown children, and am working in the securities industry.

OFFICE
SCHOOL
WORK
WHY ME?
Edith
6/29/91

SORROW/DESPAIR

BY MAYA FREED

I DON'T REMEMBER THE FACTS. I DON'T REMEMBER MY STORY. I ONLY REMEMBER THE TERROR AND DESPAIR. I WAS BORN IN 1940 IN VITEBSK, USSR AFTER MY PARENTS ESCAPED THE WARSAW GHETTO. MY MOTHER TRIED TO GET AN ABORTION BUT COULDN'T. WHEN THE BOMBINGS STARTED WE FLED IN CATTLE CARS FURTHER EAST. THIS ACCOUNTS FOR THE ENDLESS NIGHTMARE OF TRAINS AND TERRIFYING WHISTLES. MY PARENTS LOST ME SEVERAL TIMES. MY FATHER LEFT FOR PRISON. I GOT VERY SICK AND ALMOST DIED. MY MOTHER LEFT ME AT AN ORPHANAGE FOR FOUR MONTHS. SHE WAS SICK AND MY FATHER HAD MALARIA. AT AGE TWO I STOPPED WALKING, TALKING AND EATING. WHEN THEY GOT ME BACK I WAS ALMOST DEAD. ENDLESS DAYS AND WEEKS OF STARVATION AND ABANDONMENT. 1946 IN POLAND WE STAYED SEVERAL MONTHS AND LEFT BECAUSE THE POLES WERE STILL SHOOTING JEWS. WE WERE SMUGGLED INTO A WEST BERLIN REFUGEE CAMP FOR FOUR YEARS WHEN MY PARENTS BECAME ABUSIVE AND FREQUENTLY ABANDONED ME.

My parents, Morris and Blanche Rosenfeld, escaped the Warsaw ghetto in 1939-1940 in the underground. I was born in transit, ending up in Vitebsk, Bejelo Russia. Most of my relatives on both sides died in the Warsaw ghetto. When Germany invaded Russia, we continued running, hiding, travelling on trains further east to Mebekistan. In 1946, we came to Poland where again we were victims of another program, after which we were smuggled to the displaced persons camp Templehof in West Berlin where we lived for three years. By then, I had been abandoned so many times and traumatized by the war that I was unable to attend school. I only started to read at age nine, when we eventually wound up in Toronto, Canada. I am now happily married for the second time and have two wonderful adult daughters, and two adult stepsons. I am a psychotherapist.

5/91

SORROW / DESPAIR

LIFE WITH DEATH

BY ALFRED GARFINKEL

THIS PICTURE IS OF ME AND MY FEELINGS ABOUT MY MOTHER. SHE FEELS LIKE LIFE AND DEATH. HER EYES ARE LOOKING STRAIGHT OUT BUT ALSO ONLY INWARDS. THERE IS ALMOST NO FEELINGS EXPRESSED BY HER. SHE IS ALIVE BUT DEAD INSIDE. ONE HAND RESTS ON MY SHOULDER. THE OTHER DOESN'T REACH ME AND IS SLIPPING AWAY. I AM HELPLESS WITH THESE RICKETY LEGS.

I was born in the Przemysl ghetto in Poland in 1942. At eight months, my whole family was deported to Bergen Belsen where we all survived almost two-year incarceration. My father died two years ago. My mother and sister, being both widowed, live together in London.

LIFE WITH
DEATH

IF NOT FOR THEM

BY BETTY GINSBURG

THE PICTURE REPRESENTS THE DEVOTION AND LOVE MY PARENTS GAVE TO ME AND MY BROTHER WHILE WE HID DURING THE SECOND WORLD WAR. WITHOUT THEM I WOULD NOT BE HERE TO DRAW THIS PICTURE. I BELIEVE THAT I SURVIVED IN ORDER TO DO SOMETHING THAT WILL CONTRIBUTE TO THE BETTERMENT OF THE WORLD EITHER DIRECTLY OR POSSIBLY THROUGH MY CHILDREN OR GRANDCHILDREN. THROUGH THE SUFFERING AND DEGRADATION OF ALL THOSE WHO PERISHED, THE JEWISH PEOPLE CAME THROUGH STRONGER AND MORE DETERMINED TO SHOW THE WORLD THAT WE CANNOT BE BEATEN, AND THAT OUR PEOPLE WILL ALWAYS BE HERE.

I was born in a village called Klebanowka, located in the Polish part of the Ukraine. When the Germans occupied our area in 1941, there were many raids on Jews which we survived by hiding. In 1942, we were put in a ghetto in a town called Trembowlia. My mother, dressed as a Ukrainian, got out of the ghetto. Some friendly Ukrainians told her that the ghetto will be liquidated in days. She came back and told the other people about it. My parents took me and my brother and ran away from the ghetto. Her sister-in-law and her family didn't want to leave.

The ghetto was soon liquidated. The people were put on trucks and taken away to the graves to be shot. My mother saw her sister-in-law and children being put on a truck. She would always cry when recalling that incident. My father had many friends in his village and was able to hide in different places without being given away. It was very difficult for them. I was three years old and learned to be quiet and not to cry. My brother was six years old.

We all managed to survive. We were liberated by the Russians in the Summer of 1944.

Betty Ginsburg
6/29/91
If Not For Them

DEATH TRAIN TO SOBIBOR

BY LEON GINSBURG

THE LAST YEAR OF THE WAR I LIVED AS A CATHOLIC. I PASTURED MY COWS WITH THE OTHER CHRISTIAN BOYS NEAR A RAILROAD TRACK IN CHELM, NOT FAR FROM SOBIBOR. ONE DAY A TRAIN WAS STOPPED NEAR US. I WAS NEAR THE LAST WAGON. A YOUNG BOY AND GIRL WERE PUSHED AGAINST THE BACK WINDOW, THEIR EYES WIDE OPEN LOOKING STRAIGHT AT ME. I TRIED NOT TO LOOK. I WAS OVERCOME WITH FRIGHT. I DID NOT WANT THE POLISH BOYS TO NOTICE ANY REACTION ON MY FACE.

I was born in a small town called Maciejow in Eastern Poland - Volinia - now part of the Ukraine. In 1941, the Germans occupied our town. Life for the Jews became very difficult. There was a 6 p.m. curfew every night. There were periodic round-ups of Jews during which many were captured and killed.

In August of 1942, the final liquidation started. We hid in a large basement but were discovered. My mother helped me hide behind some boards just before she was stabbed by Ukrainian militiamen. I later got away from there. I found another hiding place. There were six other people there. After a few weeks, that place was found. I jumped out of a window just before the Ukrainians got inside. I got out of town and made my way to the next town - Luboml, where we had many relatives. A few days later my brother showed up. He was captured and taken to a synagogue from where they were going to take them to lime mines to be shot. He told me about the names inscribed on the walls. My sister wrote on the wall "my dear brothers take revenge" signed - Blumele Ginsburg - in Yiddish. Before they took the people to be shot my brother and another boy crawled into an oven. He pushed himself into the chimney area. A Ukrainian militiaman searched the oven and shot into it. The other boy was killed. My brother was shot in the foot. He got out in the middle of the night and came to Luboml. We slept that night holding each other. He told me he would never leave me again.

October 1, 1942, the final liquidation of Luboml started. We got into a hiding place with other relatives. Several days later the place was captured. I heard voices yelling in German "Rauss" - get out. My brother and I managed to get away by jumping out through a window and got into another house. We were hiding in an attic. That night my brother went to look for food. I never saw him again. My brother, Hershel-Zwi was 13 years old. My sister was 15.

DEATH TRAIN TO SOBIBOR

A HOLE IN A STABLE ON A POLISH FARM

BY LEA GOODMAN (APELZON)

MARCH 1944 POLISH/SLOVAK BORDER: A GROUP OF JEWS INCLUDING MY MOTHER AND MYSELF EN ROUTE INTO SLOVAKIA WERE HIDDEN IN A HOLE COVERED BY A PLANK OF WOOD AND STRAW. THE FARMER TOOK ME INTO HIS HOUSE TO SHARE HIS DAUGHTER'S BED, BUT AS HIS WIFE WAS AWAY HIS DAUGHTER LEFT ME TO JOIN HIM. AS MY FATHER HAD BEEN CAUGHT BY THE GERMANS, I WAS UPSET TO THE POINT OF PREFERRING TO GO BACK TO MY MOTHER IN THE HOLE WHERE I SPENT A CRAMPED SECOND NIGHT. I COULD NOT BEAR THE FACT THE DAUGHTER JOINED HER FATHER. I DID NOT HAVE ONE BY THEN.

Born 1935 in Cracow. Only child. 1941 - moved to Dzialoszyce with parent. At eve of deportation, family left for Koscie Camp, near Cracow, run by a friendly German called Strauss. When children could no longer be kept at the camp, I was taken to a Christian family who were the only people who kept me without payment. Thereafter I was moved to another family where my mother joined me after my father was arrested by the Germans. We were then hunted from one hiding place to another until we heard of an underground channel through Slovakia to Hungary. On our first attempt we were abandoned by a guide in the Tatra mountains, but then crossed successfully in March 1944 and reached the town of Kezmarok. The guide found mother work as a Polish Christian mother's helper with the family of a farmer/policeman of 'Volksdeutscher' origin. We remained with them until the end of the war. Shortly after the liberation by the Russians we moved to Prague and Easter 1946 left for France. My mother remarried and gave me a sister in 1948.

In 1954 I married my husband Dennis, whose German Jewish parents were murdered by the Germans, just as my own father was. Since then I have lived happily in London and have three married children with grandchildren all in London. I work in my artist's studio and mainly sculpt in metals.

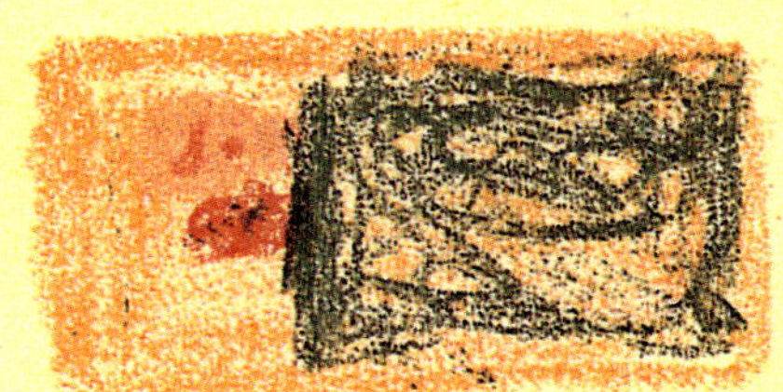

JEWISH POOL OF GENES

BY HENRY GROSSMAN

THE ELIMINATION OF A PEOPLE.

THE ELIMINATION OF THE JEWISH PEOPLE.

MEN, WOMEN, CHILDREN, LITTLE BABIES, PREGNANT WOMEN, GRANDPARENTS, COMMUNITIES, CITIES AND THE WHOLE JEWISH WORLD. CRUELTY PERSONIFIED BY A PEOPLE WHO SUPPOSEDLY BELIEVED IN GOD AND HAD SUPPOSEDLY CHRISTIAN CHARITY.

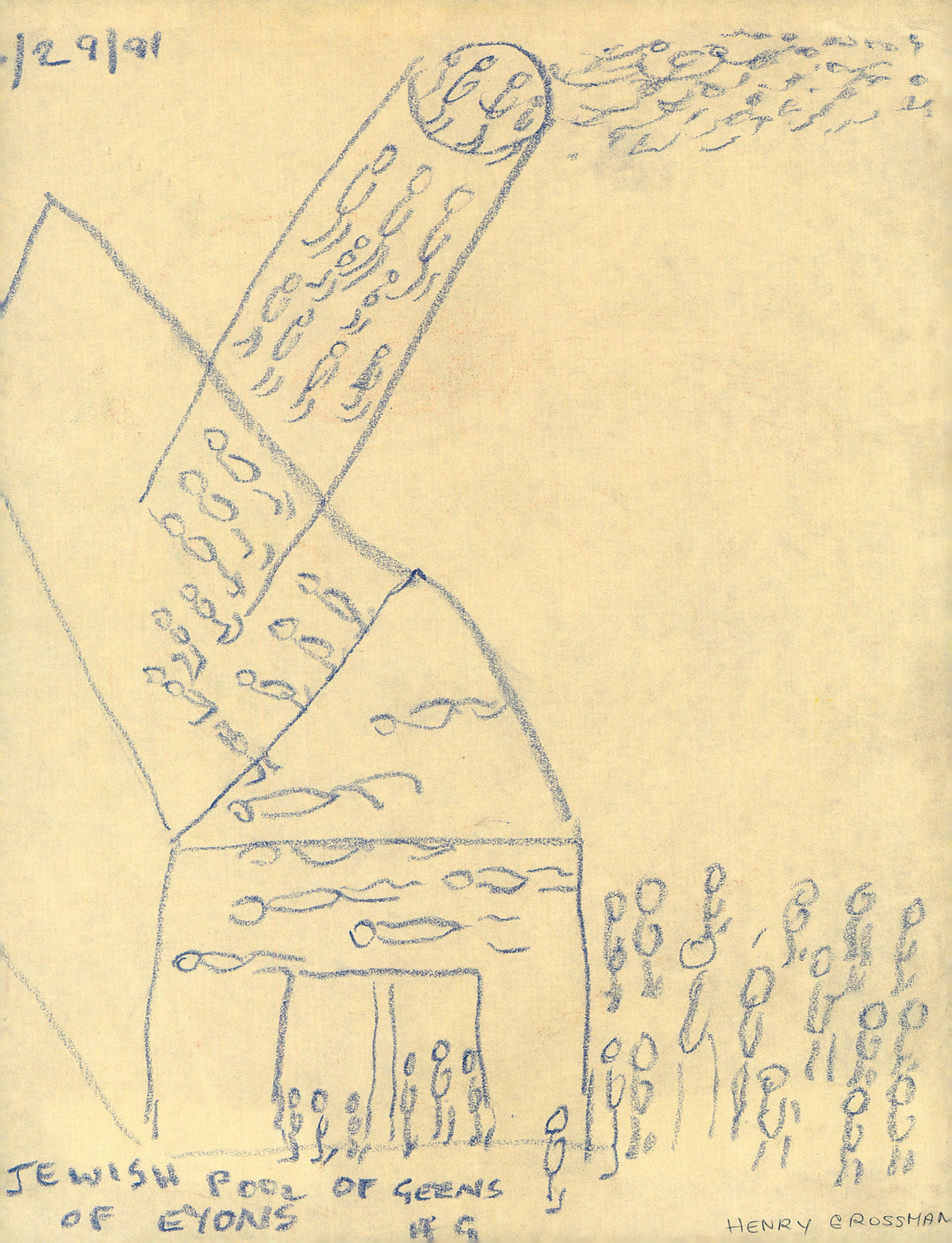
-12 9 91
JEWISH POOL OF GERMS
OF EYONS
6
HENRY GROSSMAN

IT COULD HAVE BEEN ME

BY FRAN GRUBER

I WAS BORN IN VILNO, POLAND, 1939. IN A WAY I AM ONE OF THE LUCKY ONES AS I DON'T REMEMBER THE BEGINNING, BUT THE END. THE END, OR BETTER SAID, WHEN I WAS OLD ENOUGH TO REMEMBER, WAS A TERRIBLE FEAR - A MIND FILLED WITH THINGS ABOUT GETTING CAUGHT. LIKE THE PICTURE I DREW, THE VILLAINS CAUGHT AND KILLED CHILDREN IN THE WOODS BY HANGING, WHILE I WAS LUCKILY HIDDEN IN A HOUSE OR BARN BY POLISH PEOPLE.

6/29/91

IT COULD HAVE BEEN ME

FRAN GRUBER

WE ARE SITTING AROUND A BARE TABLE

BY HANS GUGGENHEIM

WASHINGTON, JUNE 1991. WE ARE SITTING AROUND A BARE TABLE: NO CANDLES, NO MATZAH, NO SYMBOLS. THIS IS A DIFFERENT KIND OF SEDER. WE ARE HERE TO REMEMBER OUR OWN EXODUS.

TAMARA ASKS US TO CREATE OUR OWN IMAGES AND SYMBOLS. SHE WANTS US TO DRAW THEM ON PIECES OF PAPER, THEN TALK ABOUT WHY OUR PERSONAL NIGHT IS DIFFERENT FROM ALL OTHER NIGHTS, HOW WE EXPERIENCE OUR OWN EXODUS AS DIFFERENT FROM ALL OTHERS, PAST PRESENT AND FUTURE.

SOME OF US HAVE ACCESS TO OUR OWN FEELINGS - WE CAN DIP INTO OUR OWN CHILDHOOD AND FISH OUT MEMORIES.

SOME OF US FIND OUR PAST CLOSED. MY POOL IS EMPTY. I DRAW A BLANK. I MUST FEED ON THE PAST OF OTHERS.

IN NOVEMBER I RETURN TO AUSCHWITZ. I THINK: I WILL ALWAYS COME BACK HERE, ALWAYS TRY TO DRAW THE SAME THINGS: THE EYEGLASSES, TWISTED AND NOW NEARLY OPAQUE; THE TOOTHBRUSHES, AND THE SHOES. AND OF COURSE THE PIECES OF LUGGAGE WITH THE NAMES OF CHILDREN WHO TOOK THE WRONG TRAIN, WHO CAN REMEMBER NOTHING AND WHO DEPEND ON US TO REMEMBER.

I WONDER: WHEN WE CROSSED THE RED SEA, WAS ANY JEW LEFT BEHIND IN EGYPT? DID ALL THE ISRAELITES GET OUT? WHY HAVE WE COVERED WITH SILENCE WHAT HAPPENED TO THOSE WHO DID NOT MAKE IT?

Born April 1924, Berlin, Germany. November 9, 1938 - I find out about Kristallnacht the morning of November 10 and leave for the Zickel Schule, filled with anxiety. My father is being hunted by the Gestapo. November 11 - my mother sends a telegram to relatives in England who invite my sister and myself. January 1939 - we leave for England on Kindertransports. April 1940 - my parents leave for Guatemala. April 14, 1941 - I am interned as an enemy alien and sent to the Isle of Man. August 1941 - released from camp and sent, together with my sister, to Guatemala. Our convoy suffers a U-boat attack, but our ship escapes. We are interned, briefly, in Cuba. 1945 - we hear about my grandmother's death at Theresienstadt and about my father's brother's death at Auschwitz. I leave for New York. 1993 - my mother, 96, lives in New York; my sister, Gaby Strauss, in Paramus. I live in Boston. My son, Paul, attends Ithaca College.

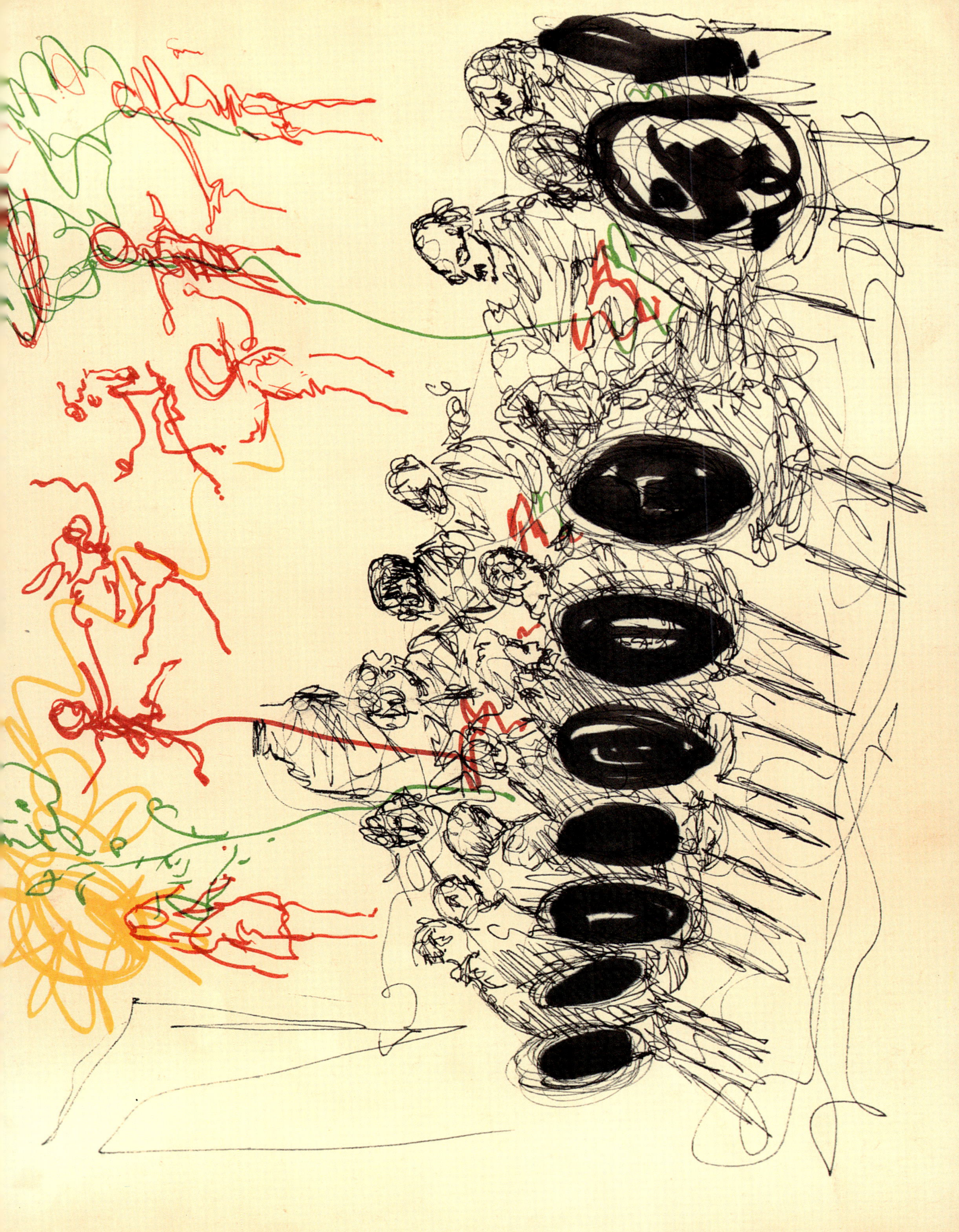

DEAR GRANDFATHER
BY TAMAR HENDEL

DEAR GRANDFATHER,
I FEEL YOUR SPIRIT AROUND AND ABOUT ME. I FEEL THE SUPPORT OF YOUR GIFT TO ME AS A CHILD, HOLDING ME UP ON THIS GREEN APPLE WORLD.
I BUILT MY JEWISH HOUSE UPON A STRONG FOUNDATION OF YOUR LOVE. I WAS THE "APPLE OF YOUR EYE."
THERE ARE NO CHIMNEYS ON THE HOUSES THAT LIVE ON THIS WORD. EACH HAS A FEATHER ON ITS DEFIANT ROOF, PROCLAIMING MIR ZEINEN DO!

My history is full of war and dislocation even before I was born. My father's family lost their livelihood and their home in Poland after WWI. My father arrived in Yugoslavia via Palestine in 1925 as a young man. The money he sent back to his parents helped support them. They, his two brothers, and three sisters, and their families, perished during the Holocaust. My mother and her family are also from Poland. They came to Yugoslavia as a result of the Austro-Hungarian War. My grandfather was conscripted as a soldier and was stationed in Zagreb, where eventually, I was born.

Perhaps it is because of my father's experience with war that he had the foresight and the courage to take us out of Yugoslavia when he did, into hiding in Italy where we survived. As a result of our timely departure, my parents were also able to save several cousins and other relatives.

We arrived in the USA in August 1944, part of the only transport of its kind to be allowed to enter before the end of WWII.

I was fortunate to survive with my immediate family intact, and to have my parents live into old age. I now live in Washington, D.C. with my husband and my children, and enjoy a satisfying career as an art therapist.

TOGETHER AGAIN

BY AMICHAI HEPPNER

MICHAEL AND I WITH OUR PARENTS RAN FROM THE CITY AND HID TOGETHER ... AND SEPARATELY. I WAS EIGHT. HE WAS SIXTEEN. WE COULD HAVE BECOME FRIENDS, WHEN WE WERE OLDER. HE COULD HAVE BEEN MY BIG BROTHER.

BUT HE WAS SEIZED AND KILLED.
IT COULD HAVE BEEN ME.
BUT IT WAS YOU.
KILLED FOR NO CAUSE EXCEPT IT WAS YOU.
NOW WE CAN BE TOGETHER AGAIN.
FOR NO CAUSE. FOR NO PURPOSE.
EXCEPT TO BE ME AND YOU.

My parents, Albert and Irene Heppner, fled from Nazi Germany shortly before my birth in 1933. We started a new life in Amsterdam; however, the Nazis stormed into the Netherlands in 1940. In 1942, my parents and I fled into the countryside to get away from Nazi raiding parties. Our plan was to meet a group who had promised to smuggle us to Free France for five thousand guilders. We were accompanied by Heinz and Elli Graumann and their son, Michael. The escape plan went awry and the gang who was to carry us to France decided to murder us instead. A cell of the regular resistance in the South of Holland heard about our plight and offered to shelter us at the farm of Harry Janssen. While we were making our way to that shelter, the leader killed Michael Graumann. The rest of us managed to escape him, and were sheltered for two years by the Janssens, despite house searches, famine and war. Our hiding place was a small chicken house. The Allied Forces who liberated us found us weak and sick. In the aftermath, my father and Elli Graumann died. The surviving three are all resettled in the United States and are still alive today.

Again
Heppner
6-29-91

ALL KINDS OF FIRE

BY HELENE HERSCHLER

I NEVER KNEW HIM. MIGHT HAVE WANTED TO. THERE'S MOSES - HE IS NOT CONSUMED? OR THE BUSH WAS NOT CONSUMED? HE'S AT THE CENTER. I'M NOT.

THROW IN YOUR LOT WITH OTHERS AND DON'T JUDGE THEM. BE KIND. LEAVE ROOM FOR ME AND MY ANGER. USE HUMOR. LET BACK TO MYSELF BEFORE 1979. LEARN BALANCE OF CARE AND SEPARATION. LEAVE SOMETHING TO THE WORLD BESIDES A CHILD.

Born in Vienna, Austria. Left there with my family in Spring of 1939, when I was four years old. Main experience was pervasive anxiety, foreboding, and realization of helplessness of my parents. Spent my youth in the U.S. Rebelled against family lifestyle which seemed too vulnerable and ineffectual to me. "Wandered" for just about 40 years. Took on role of wife and mother at age 45. Till then, it was important to me to be "role-less." Currently am a long-term cancer survivor (14+ years), and mother of a 13 year old girl about whom I feel very good. Married to a survivor who was in hiding during the war. Survivor instinct has always, since age four, been strong in me.

All Kinds
of fire
Helene H
July

I WISH

BY GILBERTE HUNKIND

I WISHED ... THE SUN, THE MOON ...
I WISHED I COULD BE THE "OTHERS"
I SEE THE CHILD THAT WAS
THE CHILD THAT <u>IS</u>
<u>TOMORROW</u> IS THE FUTURE
<u>FULL CIRCLE</u> - THE FUTURE IS BRIGHT
<u>THE BEST</u>

WISH

PAST...

PRESENT.....

~~FUTURE~~

FUTURE!

AND FOR THE "OTHERS" !?
YOU ALSO LOOK THE SAME.!?
I WISHED I COULD BE THE
"OTHERS".....

GILBERTE 6/29/91

IT COULD HAVE BEEN ME, INSTEAD IT WAS "YOU"

AND

THEY WERE AT MT. SINAI TO RECEIVE THE TORAH AND SO WAS I

BY ZELDA NUSS

I FIND THAT I HAVE TO BE A GOOD JEW, THAT I HAVE TO DO THINGS VERY HONESTLY, ETHICALLY AND MORALLY. TO SHOW THE WORLD THAT JEWS ARE GOOD HONORABLE PEOPLE. I WILL CARRY ON FOR "YOU."

I am a Child of Survivors, a Child Survivor, a hidden child. I was born in Poland to Rifka and Moishe Mirurilstein, December 1935, and have an older brother, Noah. Our life was one of a close relationship with an extended family - a grandmother, aunts, uncles, cousins, in the Wolyner-Guberne area.

When the Nazi planes started bombing and strifing our town, our little family with the expertise of my father's knowledge of the forests (he was a forester in pre-war), led us into hiding.

The survival game was full of fear and reprieve. Safety was completely in my parents hands.

My parents are not with us anymore, but they still live in the hearts of the lives they touched and rescued. The beat and courage of their tender hearts is a standard to the strength of Jewish history.

I am very lucky. I remember the many horrors, but I will never forget the strength of Rifka and Moishe ... my mother and father. The child within me is still hearing and finding safety to the sound of their heartbeats.

6-29-91

Zelda (Mirmilstein) Nuss

HIDING & FIGHTING
BY HELEN ROTHSTEIN

WHERE WAS GOD LOOKING DOWN WHILE CHILDREN OF INNOCENT PEOPLE WERE KILLED?

I was born in a little town in Poland, Wyszkow/NB about 50 km from Warsaw. When the war started in September 1939, I was not quite ten years old. My town was leveled by the Germans.

The first wave of Germans rounded up all the Jews in the town, shepherded them into the synagogue, set it on fire, and burned everyone alive. I had many relatives among them.

My parents, brother, sister and myself were hiding in a bunker. When we came out we were rounded up. The Jews were separated from the Polish non-Jews. They were allowed to have some potatoes and water. The Jews were given nothing, since they were digging their own graves, but didn't know it at the time, until a German soldier, he was a Wermaht officer, told us that he was giving us a gift of life and we should leave immediately and never return.

My father gave me some money and I went to Warsaw to obtain Polish documents for my family. I returned to Brzuza to tell my family what happened to me. Unfortunately, I found out the Germans had staged a raid and rounded up as many Jews as they could find, my mother and sister among them. They killed them on the spot. My father, with a broken heart and tears in his eyes, insisted that I, at the age of thirteen, leave him and save my life. That was the last time I saw my father and brother alive.

I found a job on a farm as a maid until the end of 1944. I decided to hitchhike back to the village of Brzuza, hoping to find my father and brother alive; but instead I was left all alone without any hope at the age of fifteen, in a country that decided even the few Jews who survived were too many for them. After the war, the Vojska Krajova were killing Jews wherever they could find them. My aunt and cousin, who were saved in Russia, returned to Poland in 1945 and were killed. A few of my friends in Lochov were killed.

In December 1947, I received my visa for the United States. My mother's uncle sponsored me so that I would not become a ward of the United States.

I chose not to date Holocaust survivors so that I should not have to talk about our different experiences and how we managed to survive. In 1948 I met a very nice young man who was just discharged from the service and fell in love with him. We were married on July 10, 1949. We have four children. Each one is named after my beloved family, my mother, father, sister and brother.

No one who did not go through the Holocaust could ever imagine the devastation we carry with us for the rest of our lives.

6/29/91
6/29/43
In Hiding and fighting

MY MOTHER HOLDING ME AS A BABY

BY JOHANNA SAPER

AT FIRST I DREW A PICTURE OF MY MOTHER HOLDING ME AS A BABY. MY MOTHER IS VERY WARM AND VERY SOFT. THE BABY IS CONTENT. IN THE NEXT SEQUENCE I AM ALONE, ABANDONED WITH MY HEAD DOWN, CRYING. MY MOTHER IS GONE, I AM A CHILD ALONE. AFTER CONTEMPLATING THE TWO IMAGES, I ADDED A THIRD PERSON. HE IS STRONG AND HE HAS A PURPOSE IN HIS LIFE, HE CAN LAUGH AND TELL JOKES AND HE SAVED ME FROM LONELINESS. HE IS MY HUSBAND.

I was born in Vienna, Austria, the youngest of three children. In 1938 I was ten years old. When the Nazis marched into Austria, everything changed drastically and rapidly for our family. My father's business was taken over; I could no longer attend the gymnasium, my brother was put on a "work detail." The S.S. came into our house and took everything of value. Through an ad, which my parents placed in an English newspaper, I was able to leave for England and live with a family there. The farewell party at the airport included aunts, uncles, friends and my parents. It was the last time I saw any of them. Shortly after I arrived in England the war started and we spent many frightening nights and days in air-raid shelters. I arrived in the United States just before the war started here. I have never found out where or how my mother perished and have mourned and missed her all my life.

Johanna Shape
6-29-91

THEN & NOW

BY AVA SCHONBERG

THE SMALL FIGURE IS ME AS A CHILD AND THE LARGE PICTURE IS ME NOW. THE BLACK SPACE AND SMALL HOLE IS A DARK PERIOD AND VERY LITTLE MEMORY. THE YELLOW AND ORANGE SPACE WAS A PERIOD OF HOPE AFTER THE WAR. THE LARGE RED HOLE IS THE HOLE IN MY MEMORY NOW ABOUT MY CHILDHOOD AND ALL THE THINGS THAT I LOST OF THAT PERIOD IN MY LIFE.

I was born in Antwerp, Belgium, and I have two sisters. I am the middle one. In September, 1941, when I was four years old, the Gestapo took my father away and we never saw him again. We went into hiding and were hidden in many different places near Brussels. In 1943 my mother was able to put me and my older sister in a convent in Weerenbeek. In early 1944, the Belgium underground smuggled in a truck, me and my little sister who was two years old into Switzerland. My mother and older sister came later. In Zurich I was put in a foster home. After the war my mother took us back to Belgium. I stayed in an orphanage for two years, while my mother got her life together. In 1950 my mother remarried. In 1954 we came to the U.S. I am alone in New York now. My mother and stepfather went to live in Israel and they are both dead now. My younger sister lives in Belgium. My older one in Boston. The rest of my family was killed by the Germans.

THEN AND NOW

AVA '91

THE LEGACY

BY DANA SCHWARTZ

I'VE BEEN LEFT. THEY TOUCH MY SHOULDER TO SAY GOODBYE AND SOMEHOW TO LET ME KNOW THAT THE BROKEN WORLD IS UP TO ME TO FIX NOW. I LOOK SADLY AT THE TOOLS. I CONTEMPLATE THE TOOLS, WONDERING:

WHICH ONES SHALL I USE?

WHICH ONE AM I MOST CAPABLE OF USING?

WILL ANYTHING HELP?

IS THERE ANY USE?

I CHOSE TO USE THEM. I'LL TRY.

I CHOSE LIFE BUT I MISS THEM SO.

I was born in Lvov, Poland. I was in a ghetto with my parents and we hid under our building in a hole during actions. I've also hidden in attics, behind stairs and in the forest. (It's hard to talk about where I hid. I guess I don't want to be found out.)

Father paid a man to take us to his village and say that we were his cousin's wife and child. No one there knew we were Jews, but we were very frightened. We stayed on our haystack mattress most of the time, because it was safer and warmer. Mother taught me to recite ancient Greek poetry by heart as I stuck my freezing toes between her legs for warmth. (I made a lot of deals with God.) Only she and I survived. We came to America and she died, leaving me orphaned but in a country where everything is possible. I've made a beautiful new family. (I'm a psychotherapist and I work with children.)

DANA

WHERE IS EVERYONE GOING

BY ELLEN SHER

I FELT LEFT OUT. EVERYONE SEEMS TO HAVE DIRECTION. THEY ARE GOING SOMEWHERE - ACHIEVING -INVOLVED - HAVE PURPOSES. I WANT TO GO TOO BUT NEVER SEEM TO FIT IN. ALWAYS A SPECTATOR, NEVER REALLY AN HONEST PARTICIPANT.

Where is Everyone going??

ELLEN SHER (ALTENBERG)

6-29-91

JOURNEY

BY MAURICE SINGER

I HAVE BEGUN MY "JOURNEY" FROM LEFT GOING RIGHT IN THE HEBREW AND YIDDISH WAY OF WRITING. I AM THAT PERSON ON WHOSE HEAD AIRPLANES ARE DROPPING BOMBS. THE WAR OVER, MY FAMILY AND I CAME TO AMERICA PASSING THE STATUE OF LIBERTY. FROM BOTTOM TO TOP MY MAJOR LOCATIONS: NEW YORK CITY, BROCKTON-BOSTON, THE HOUSE I LIVED IN AND THE PRESENT.

I was born in Antwerp, Belgium in 1938. Our family lived there until we heard about the roundup of Jews, after the Germans conquered Belgium. We then moved to a smaller town La Louviere, also in Belgium. We were in hiding, always one step ahead of a couple of roundups, from one apartment to another. My parents could not care for all of us, so my brother and I were sent to a convent. After some excessive bombing which hit and demolished part of the convent, my parents took us back. We then moved to a still smaller town called Thieu where we lived for the last 2-1/2 years of the war. While there, I witnessed an early German rocket, the V-2, flying overhead on its way to England. I also witnessed the German's retreat and the allies' advance. When the war was declared over, we returned to Antwerp and lived there until 1947. My father's brothers in the United States sponsored our emigration here. We arrived in January 1948. I am married, have no children. I work as a ritual director at Adas Israel in Washington, D.C. I am very involved in promoting Yiddish music and the Yiddish language.

JOURNEY
MAURICE
1991
D.C.
BROCKTON
BOSTON

ONLY ONE GOT AWAY

BY ELEANOR TANNENHOLZ SOBEL

THE BARBED WIRE IS CLOSING ON A FAMILY AND A MEMBER GETS TANGLED AND STABBED, ANOTHER DIES FROM FRIGHT WHILE THE MOTHER BIRD, TO THE LEFT, MOURNS AND THE FATHER BIRD IN THE CENTER SCREAMS FOR THE FLEDGLING BIRD TO ESCAPE.

THERE IS JOY THAT ONE ESCAPED. BUT THERE IS HORROR THAT CAN NEVER BE LEFT BEHIND.

I am the spouse of Nathan Sobel, a survivor. Nathan calls me a Yankee Doodle - I'm a fourth generation American and yet he knows I feel a very strong affiliation with European, as well as American Jews, and with Israel as well as the stamp of the Holocaust.

Living with a Holocaust survivor can mean almost anything, but in my situation, it means lots of creative involvement.

Living with a survivor has meant being a Sherlock Holmes at anti-Semitism, sniffing it out, expressing outrage - lots of anger - a counter commentary to ignorance.

6/29/91
Only One
Got Away!

FREEDOM NO!

BY NAT SOBEL

THE YEARS 1941 TO 1944 WERE THE DARKEST YEARS IN MY LIFE. AS IT TURNED OUT IT WAS THE DARKEST PERIOD IN THE HISTORY OF HUMAN-KIND. MORE INNOCENT PEOPLE WERE KILLED DURING THAT PERIOD IN MASS-PRODUCTION THAN IN ANY OTHER TIME IN HISTORY ... AND THE PEOPLE TURNED OUT TO BE MY PEOPLE.

I FELT THE LONELIEST CHILD ON EARTH. FOR A LONG PERIOD I THOUGHT I WAS THE VERY LAST JEW ON EARTH. TO BE THE VERY LAST OF ANYTHING IS VERY SCARY AND VERY HAUNTING. THE SUN, RAINBOW AND THEREFORE FREEDOM, WERE BARRED FOR ME. DARK CLOUDS HOVERED OVER ME. I, SO VERY YOUNG, SO VERY LITTLE, SO INSIGNIFICANT, WAS VERY PROUD OF MY YELLOW STAR. IT WAS FOR ME A BADGE OF HONOR.

I am the sole survivor of my immediate family of six. The rest of the extended family of about 45 members were also annihilated during the Holocaust by the German, Ukrainian and Polish Nazis. I was born in Eastern Poland near the Ukraine. I escaped from the ghetto and was running and hiding in about 42 places for several years until the liberation by the Russian army. I ran across borders and countries until I reached Berlin in 1945. I was included in the first group of 43 child survivors to leave Europe for Palestine via France with the Children's Aliyah in 1946. I participated in the Israeli War of Independence in the Haganah and in the Army and came to the United States in 1952. I attended Brooklyn College and Columbia University. I was employed by New York City as a city planner and Director or Urban Renewal. I have authored eight books on Planning and Housing in New York City, including a two-volume atlas. I am an inventor, a designer of medals, a frustrated artist, a founder and editor of The Shekel, an international Judaic Numismatic hobby magazine. I conceived the Shoa Haggadah and am involved with many groups and organizations. I am married to Eleanor and have two sons from a previous marriage.

Nat Sobel
Freedom...
BARRED
1941-44
Me, a very little Jewish Boy
My Yellow Badge
FREEDOM NO!

TRIUMPH OVER GUILT

BY TRUDI ALEXY STERNLICHT

I SURVIVED THE HOLOCAUST BY BECOMING A CATHOLIC AND LIVING A LIE. FOR YEARS I FELT ENORMOUS GUILT. EVERY TIME I REACHED OUT FOR SOMETHING I HEARD GOD CALLING ME A LIAR AND AN IMPOSTOR, TELLING ME I SHOULD BE DEAD AND HAVE NO RIGHT TO BE HAPPY. ONLY RECENTLY I HAVE BROKEN THROUGH THE BARRIER OF GUILT AND HAVE RECONNECTED TO MY JEWISH ROOTS. I AM A DOUBLE SURVIVOR: I SURVIVED THE HOLOCAUST, AND I SURVIVED THE DEATH OF MY SOUL.

Born in Rumania in 1927, I lived in Prague, Czechoslovakia for eight years, until 1938, when our thoroughly assimilated Jewish family moved to Paris. When war broke out in 1939, we fled to Spain, as hastily baptized Catholics. During our two years in Barcelona, I fell under the spell of Catholic ritual. When we moved to the U.S., I was sent to a Catholic high school and later won a scholarship to a Catholic college.

With the rise of Israel, news of the death camps, and ever-increasing religious doubts, long dormant guilt over my survival by fraud grew. I felt by becoming a Catholic I had forfeited my right to be a Jew. I quit college in my junior year, married in haste and bore two children whom we raised as Unitarians until our daughter asked to join a friend attending a Jewish Sunday school. This finally allowed me to acknowledge my Jewish roots openly and confront my guilt in therapy. It took years before I felt I could call myself a Jew.

Eventually, I discovered a profound kinship with Spain's Secret Jews, the Marranos, who also converted under duress during the medieval Inquisition.

I recently published a book, THE MEZUZAH IN THE MADONNA'S FOOT, ORAL HISTORIES EXPLORING 500 YEARS IN THE PARADOXICAL RELATIONSHIP OF SPAIN AND THE JEWS, (Simon and Schuster, author name listed as Trudi Alexy). I recently joined a rather unorthodox Jewish congregation and now live my life as a Jew.

TRiOMPH OVER GUILT

TEDDi STERNLiCHT

6/28/91

ANCSIKA MY LOVELY BROTHER: IT COULD HAVE BEEN ME

BY HEDY VAN WHY

MY GRANDMOTHER AND MY LITTLE BROTHER WENT HAND IN HAND TO THE "LEFT" WHEN WE GOT TO AUSCHWITZ. I AM STILL HOPEFUL THAT ANCSIKA, MY BROTHER, WILL COME BACK. AM I DREAMING? I WISH FOR HIS MIRACULOUS RETURN? HE WAS SUCH A BEAUTIFUL CHILD, JUST BAR-MITZVAHED ... HE HAD A LOVELY VOICE. I NEVER SAID GOOD BYE TO HIM OR MY GRANDMOTHER, THAT WONDERFUL EARTH MOTHER ...

I was born in Sighet, Romania, in 1929. When I was ten years old, the Germans attacked Poland and many refugees came across the borders. That was my first encounter with the war.

When I was fourteen, we lived in Nagyszollos, Hungary. The Germans put us in a ghetto from April through May 1944. My grandmother, Regina Rosner; my parents, Emil and Kornel Rosner - ne Tabak; my only brother, Ancsika, and I were taken to Auschwitz. We arrived on my father's 39th birthday, June 4th. My mother and I worked in an airplane factory. Father barely made it, grandmother and Ancsika marched to the <u>left</u> - never to be seen again ...

In May of 1945, the Russians liberated us. My mother and I went back to Nagyszollos. Later, my father joined us.

I'm still mourning for my brother, three grandparents, fourteen aunts and uncles, eleven cousins, and all my Jewish friends and schoolmates.

I have a grown daughter and three grandchildren. I live alone.

Ancsika
my lovely
brother: it
could of
be me.....
Spring of 1944
my dear
grand-
mother
REGINA
saying good
by to her favorite
HEDY
6/1991
ROSNER-VAN WHY

ONE DAY I'LL BE FIRST

BY RAE WEITZ

I SOMEHOW NEVER WANT TO THINK OF, OR CONSIDER, MYSELF.

EVERYTHING AND EVERYBODY COMES FIRST.

WHEN IT'S TIME TO END, WHICH OBVIOUSLY REFERS TO MY LIFE AS WELL, I SUDDENLY REMEMBER THAT I EXIST. BY THEN, THERE ISN'T MUCH ROOM FOR ME; OR TIME TO EXPAND ON MY LIFE.

BUT ONE DAY, I'M SURE I WILL BE PRESENT.

I WISH A LOT, BUT IT'S BURIED VERY DEEP.

ONE DAY I'LL COME FIRST.

After my father was killed, in 1942, Mother found a place in a nearby village where the three of us, (I have a younger sister), hid until the end of the war.

When the woman, in who's place we were hiding, realized that this was not going to be as short a time as we expected, she wanted us to leave. Since mother refused, she did everything to make it difficult for us so we would be forced to leave. But there was no place to go.

It would've been easy for her to have us taken away, but she was afraid that the other villagers would find out that she was hiding Jews, and this would've been a terrible shame.

Besides going out on dark nights to gather some apples and potatoes, left in the ground after the harvest, we got some help from three men who were hiding in a nearby village. One of them was killed by Poles after the war.

We now live in New York City. Mother died in 1983.

One day I'll be first
Now my wishes are buried deep.

Survivor Group Contact Information

If you were a child during the Holocaust and you wish to become a member of a survivor's group, please print or type your name, address and telephone number and send to:

Create Expressive Arts Press
8004A Norfolk Avenue
Bethesda, Maryland 20814

We will forward the information to the appropriate groups which meet regularly in:

Los Angeles
Chicago
Philadelphia
New York City
Washington, D.C.
Boston
Miami
Montreal, Canada
and Others

To order copies of this book
photocopy and return form below.

Number of copies ______ @ $19.95

Shipping + handling ______ @ $3.00 per book

Total Enclosed $______

Please enclose check or money order.

(Please print)

Name: ____

Address: ____

____

____

Telephone:____________________ Fax:____________________

Send to: *Create Expressive Arts Press*
8004A Norfolk Avenue
Bethesda, Maryland 20814
(301) 652-2787 FAX: (301) 652-2742

Please allow 3 - 4 weeks for delivery.

For volume discounts, please write or call Create Expressive Arts Press at the above numbers.